KU-539-165

First Book of
Animals

First Book of
Animals

Steve Parker

Miles Kelly
PUBLISHING

First published in 2004 by
Miles Kelly Publishing Ltd
Bardfield Centre
Great Bardfield
Essex, CM7 4SL

Copyright © Miles Kelly Publishing 2004

Some material in this book first appeared in
Things you should know about

2 4 6 8 10 9 7 5 3 1

Publishing Director: Anne Marshall
Project Editor: Belinda Gallagher
Editorial Assistant: Rosalind McGuire
Design: HERRING BONE DESIGN/Louisa Leitao

All rights reserved. No part of this publication may be stored in a retrieval
system, or transmitted by any means, electronic, mechanical, photocopying,
recording or otherwise, without the prior permission of the copyright holder

ISBN 1-84236-447-2

Printed in Hong Kong, China, Singapore, Thailand

British Library Cataloguing-in-Publication Data
A catalogue record for this book is available from the British Library

www.mileskelly.net
info@mileskelly.net

Contents

Big Cats

Bears

Whales & Dolphins

King of the dinosaurs

Dinosaur facts

- Tyrannosaurus was 12 metres in length.
- It lived in North America.
- It was one of the last dinosaurs and lived about 65 million years ago.

TYRANNOSAURUS REX was one of the biggest hunting animals ever to walk the Earth. This massive meat-eater had more than 50 teeth — each one of them was bigger than your hand.

Dinosaur name

- Say it: 'Ty-ran-owe-saw-rus-rex'.

- It means 'king of the tyrant lizards'.

Tyrannosaurus weighed about seven tonnes — that's as heavy as two elephants.

8

The teeth of Tyrannosaurus had wavy, saw-like edges called serrations. They could easily slice through the flesh of its victim.

Even bigger!

Giganotosaurus was another meat-eating dinosaur. It was even larger than Tyrannosaurus!

The arms of Tyrannosaurus were tiny and probably useless.

9

Dinosaur facts

• Ankylosaurus lived 70 million years ago in North America.
• It was 10 metres long and weighed five tonnes.

Dinosaur name

• Say it: 'An-kill-owe-saw-rus'.
• It means 'stiff or fused lizard'.

Hammer-tailed dinosaur!

ANKYLOSAURUS had two heavy lumps of bone at the end of its tail. It could swing these at enemies like a huge hammer. But for most of the time, this dinosaur was a peaceful plant-eater.

Ankylosaurus was protected by long spikes of bone on its head • • • • • • • • • • • • *and shoulders.*

Each lump of bone on the tail was as big as a basketball.

Bony tail

The tail club of *Ankylosaurus* was made of bone, which had become stuck, or fused, together.

Pieces of bone as big as dinner plates, and very hard scales, protected the back of Ankylosaurus.

Ankylosaurus crouched down to protect its soft underside.

Hunting in packs

- Deinonychus was 1.6 metres high – as tall as a human.
- It lived in North America 110 million years ago.

**Dinosaur
name**

- Say it: 'Day-non-ee-cuss'.
- It means 'terrible claw'.

DEINONYCHUS went on the prowl in a group or pack. In this way it could attack prey much bigger than itself, like a one-tonne *Tenontosaurus*. This gave enough food for a whole week!

Some dinosaurs died and their bones, teeth and claws were preserved as fossils. The fossils of several Deinonychus were found together, showing that they lived and hunted in groups.

Deinonychus *had strong back legs.
It could run fast, jump high
and leap a
long way.*

Clever dinosaur?

The brain of Deinonychus was quite big compared to other dinosaurs. It may have been pretty clever!

Deinonychus *slashed
out with its powerful
hand claws.*

The toe of Deinonychus had a huge, curved claw. This was used to rip open its victim.

Plate-backed dinosaur

Dinosaur facts

- Stegosaurus lived about 150 million years ago in North America.
- Stegosaurus was nine metres long and weighed two tonnes.

Dinosaur name

- Say it: Steg-owe-sore-uss'.
- It means 'roof lizard'.

STEGOSAURUS had tall, thin plates of bone on its back. Why? Perhaps they soaked up the Sun's heat, to make this dinosaur warm. The hotter *Stegosaurus* got, the faster it moved.

Stegosaurus had a mouth shaped like a bird's beak, for pecking at plant food.

14

The back plates were as tall and wide as a pillow. But they were only as thick as your wrist.

Tiny brain

Stegosaurus was as big as an elephant, but its brain was as small as your thumb. So it wasn't very clever!

Caring mother

Dinosaur facts
• Maiasaura was nine metres in length.
• It lived 80 million years ago in North America.

Dinosaur name
• Say it: 'My-ah-sore-ah'.
• It means 'good mother lizard'.

The big plant-eating dinosaur **MAIASAURA** laid its eggs in a bowl-shaped nest, which it scooped in the soil. It protected the eggs from hungry enemies and even fed the babies when they hatched.

Fossils have been found of Maiasaura nests, babies and grown-ups. The nests were quite close together, in a group called a breeding colony.

The Maiasaura nest was about two metres across and contained around 20 eggs.

Each baby Maiasaura hatched from an egg about as big as your two fists placed end-to-end. Its leg bones were not quite strong enough for it to run around.

The mother Maiasaura brought leaves and berries back to the nest, for her babies to eat.

Mega eggs!

Some mother dinosaurs laid eggs 30 centimetres long — the size of a rugby ball — and as big as 50 hen's eggs.

Speedy dinosaurs

Fast-running dinosaurs like **ORNITHOMIMUS** were called 'ostrich-dinosaurs'. This is because they were very similar in size and shape to the bird of today, the ostrich. Perhaps they ran as fast, too!

Dinosaur facts

• Ornithomimus was about three metres long and lived 75 million years ago.

Dinosaur name

• Say it: 'Or-nith-owe-mim-uss'.
• It means 'like an ostrich'.

Ornithomimus *had powerful muscles in its hips and upper legs, to take long, quick strides.*

The lower legs and feet were long, slim and light.

18

The long neck of Ornithomimus helped it to peck on the ground. ....

Ornithomimus had no teeth at all! Its long, beak-shaped mouth was suited to pecking and snapping up all kinds of foods, from leaves to little lizards.

Ornithomimus *had a top speed of 80 kilometres an hour – twice as fast as a champion human sprinter.*

Fastest!

An ostrich-dinosaur or an ostrich would not quite catch the fastest runner today – the cheetah.

Noisy dinosaurs

The plant-eater **PARASAUROLOPHUS** had a long tube of bone sticking up from the back of its head. This was hollow. Perhaps the dinosaur blew air through it to make loud noises – just like an elephant does when it 'trumpets' through its trunk.

Perhaps **Parasaurolophus** *made noises to frighten off enemies. These noises may have helped to attract a mate, or warned other herd members of danger.*

Dinosaur facts

- Parasaurolophus lived 70 million years ago in North America.
- It was 10 metres from nose to tail.

Dinosaur name

- Say it: 'Pa-ra-sore-owe-loaf-uss'.
- It means 'beside ridged lizard'.

Dino-song!

Roll a card sheet into a long tube. Shout and make noises through it. Maybe that's how dinosaurs 'sang'!

Parasaurolophus breathed air in through its nose. The air passed up and down inside the hollow tube, before it went into the body.

The bony tube had no hole at the end. Its tip was sealed.

Dinosaur giant!

Dinosaur facts
- Brachiosaurus was 25 metres in length.
- It lived 140 million years ago in Africa, Europe and North America.

Dinosaur name
- Say it: 'Brack-ee-owe-sore-uss'.
- It means 'arm lizard'.

BRACHIOSAURUS was one of the biggest dinosaurs that ever lived. It weighed over 50 tonnes — more than a huge juggernaut truck. It was also one of the tallest dinosaurs. Its head could stretch to 13 metres above the ground.

Giant feet!
Brachiosaurus had huge feet and made footprints one metre across — bigger than a school desk.

Because of its huge size, Brachiosaurus must have spent its whole life eating. Its neck was more than eight metres long, the same length as a flag pole!

Brachiosaurus had a small head and peg-like teeth for pulling leaves off twigs.

The front legs, or 'arms', were longer than the back legs, adding to the great height of Brachiosaurus.

The smallest of all

Dinosaur facts
- Compsognathus lived 150 million years ago in Europe.

Dinosaur name
- Say it: 'Comp-sog-nay-thuss'.
- It means 'elegant jaw'.

COMPSOGNATHUS was just about the tiniest dinosaur. However, even though it was small, it was very fierce. *Compsognathus* was a speedy hunter of little creatures such as insects, worms — and perhaps baby dinosaurs.

Compsognathus was small and slender. It weighed only three kilograms — less than an average pet cat.

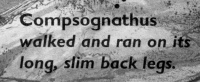

Compsognathus walked and ran on its long, slim back legs.

24

The head on the long, bendy neck could dart about and snap up prey.

Compsognathus had many small, sharp, curved teeth for biting its tiny victims.

The arms of Compsognathus had sharp claws for grabbing food.

Micro dino!

Compsognathus was about as tall as a chicken of today, but much thinner — and without the feathers.

Dinosaur horns and frills

Dinosaur facts
- Triceratops lived 65 million years ago.
- It was nine metres long and weighed five tonnes.

Dinosaur name
- Say it 'Try-sarah-tops'.
- It means 'three horns on the face'.

TRICERATOPS was usually a quiet, peaceful plant-eater. But if an enemy came near, it charged with its head down, and jabbed with its long, sharp horns. The wide frill of bone over its neck made it look even more fearsome!

Like all dinosaurs, Triceratops had tough, scaly skin.

Triceratops *had to defend itself against the great meat-eater* Tyrannosaurus. *These two dinosaurs lived at the same time in the same region.*

Shadow dino!

Put your fingers in the positions shown, between a desk lamp and the wall. See the shadowy dinosaur!

The nose horn of Triceratops *was quite short. But the horns over the eyes were more than one metre long.*

Sharks love meat!

Shark facts
- Great whites grow to over seven metres in length.
- Great whites live in warm seas and oceans around the world.
- Great whites are rare as so many have been killed by people.

Sharks hunt the meat or flesh of other animals. The **GREAT WHITE** is the biggest, fiercest hunting shark of all. It feeds on almost any prey, from small fish to great whales – and even people. The great white is also called a 'man-eater'.

The great white's teeth are up to eight centimetres – as long as a finger. And there are more than 50 of them!

Great whites are so dangerous,
divers who study and photograph
them stay in a strong safety-cage.

Jumbo shark!

The biggest great white ever
weighed was 4 ½ tonnes.
That's as heavy as
a full-grown elephant!

The great white is certainly great,
but it's not white – it has a dark grey
back, and a pale grey or cream
underside, often with dark scars from
old wounds.

Sharks cannot chew!

Shark facts
- The whale shark grows to more than 15 metres long.
- Whale sharks can weigh over 20 tonnes.

Most sharks are big. The **WHALE SHARK** is a giant! It is the world's biggest fish, but is not a fierce hunter. It swims with its mouth open, filtering small animals such as fish and krill from the water with its special comb-like gills. Like all sharks, it cannot chew — it just swallows its food whole!

The whale shark has only very small teeth in its huge mouth.

Whale sharks often lie still just under the surface of the water. Are they sunbathing or resting? No one really knows for sure.

Tiny snacks
The whale shark's food includes small fish, and shrimp-like animals called krill — each about as big as your little finger.

The whale shark has a spotty back and pale underside.

Big sharks often have smaller fish, like these pilot fish, swimming with them.

Sharks have super senses!

Shark facts
- The great hammerhead is more than five metres long.
- Sometimes hammerheads have dozens of stingray stings stuck in their throats.

Sharks like the **HAMMERHEAD** are super-sensitive. They can smell blood in the water from five kilometres away. In clear seas they can see for 30 metres ahead of them. They even sense tiny amounts of natural electricity in the water, made by their prey.

Water-wings!

The 'hammer' is like an underwater wing. It helps the shark to swim well and stay up near the surface.

The snout (nose area) detects tiny bursts of electricity in the water which are made by other animals as they move.

The eye and nostril are at the very end of the amazing lobed head.

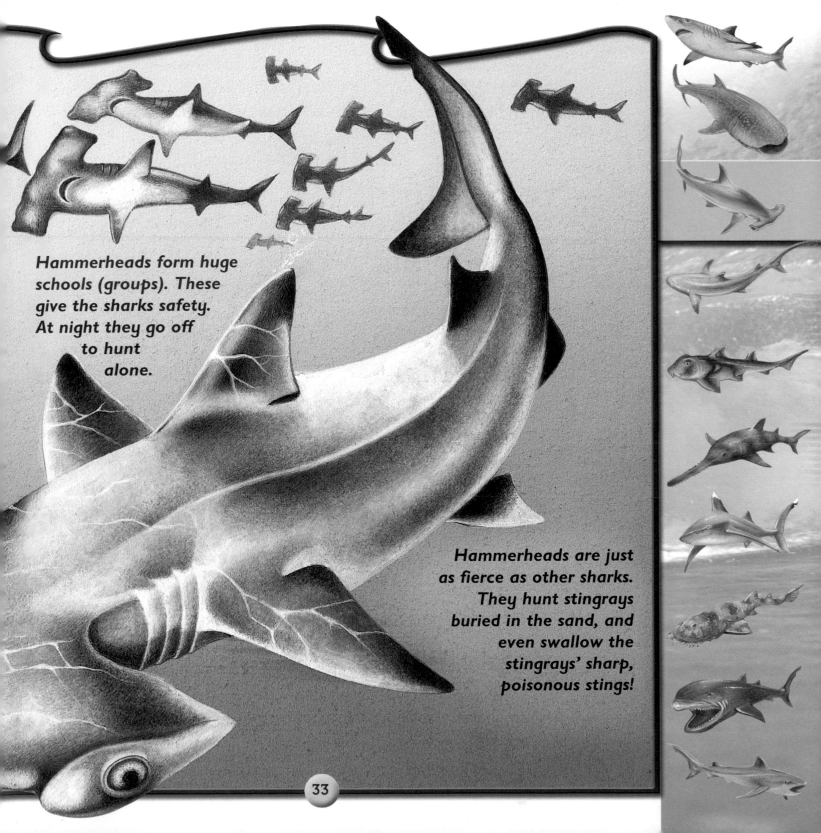

Hammerheads form huge schools (groups). These give the sharks safety. At night they go off to hunt alone.

Hammerheads are just as fierce as other sharks. They hunt stingrays buried in the sand, and even swallow the stingrays' sharp, poisonous stings!

A deadly tail!

Sharks swish their tails to and fro, to swim fast. But the **THRESHER** uses its tail in another way too — as a weapon! It flicks its long tail about like an underwater whip, bashing small fish to wound or stun them. Then the thresher snaps them up in its mouth.

Shark facts
• The thresher's tail can be three metres – half the shark's total length.
• Threshers are also called fox sharks or swingle-tails.

The thresher's teeth are small and triangle-shaped, but they're very sharp, just like short knife blades.

34

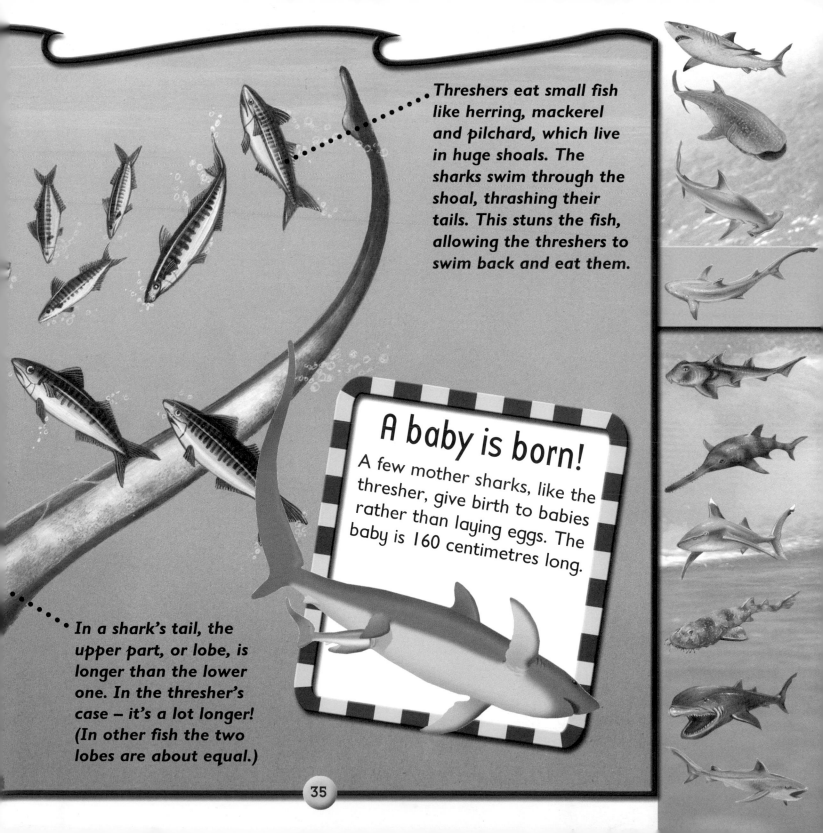

Threshers eat small fish like herring, mackerel and pilchard, which live in huge shoals. The sharks swim through the shoal, thrashing their tails. This stuns the fish, allowing the threshers to swim back and eat them.

A baby is born!

A few mother sharks, like the thresher, give birth to babies rather than laying eggs. The baby is 160 centimetres long.

In a shark's tail, the upper part, or lobe, is longer than the lower one. In the thresher's case — it's a lot longer! (In other fish the two lobes are about equal.)

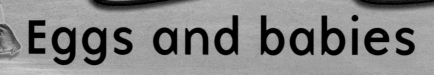

Eggs and babies

Shark facts
• Port Jackson sharks grow to two metres long.
• They gather in shallow water on rocky reefs to breed.

Some sharks lay eggs, like the mother **PORT JACKSON SHARK**. She sticks them to rocks or weeds on the seabed. A few weeks later the baby sharks hatch out. They're hardly bigger than your hand. They look just like their parents – and start to hunt straight away!

Each back fin has a sharp, pointed spine just in front of it – to act as protection against other sharks.

The eggs are attached to rocks or pebbles on the seabed.

Port Jacksons are in the group called horned or bullhead sharks. They have a horn-like ridge above each eye, and a wide, blunt head. They can lie still on the seabed for hours.

Screwy egg!

Port Jackson eggs are up to 20 centimetres long. A strange screw-shaped ridge holds the eggs among the rocks.

Small, sharp front teeth in the down pointing mouth grab shellfish, crabs, shrimps and worms. Bigger, flat rear teeth crush them.

Sharks are very scaly!

Shark facts
- The saw shark reaches about 1.2 metres in length.
- Saw sharks are related to saw fish and both have a long, saw-shaped snout.

A shark's skin is covered by small scales. These are very sharp and pointed – in fact, they are just like tiny teeth. The **SAW SHARK** also has teeth outside of its mouth. These run in a row along each side of its long snout. The saw shark 'saws' into mud and seaweed to find fish and starfish, and eats them using the teeth in its mouth.

The snout teeth look like a chainsaw and are just as dangerous.

On each side of the snout is a long, bendy feeler – a barbel. It wriggles like a finger in the mud to find food.

Be a saw shark!

You can make any kind of shark mask, from stiff card. But the saw shark looks one of the fiercest and funniest!

The saw shark has a flattened body which is ideal for lying low! It spends most of its time swimming or resting on the seabed.

Sharks like to sleep!

Shark facts
- White-tipped reef sharks are two metres in length.
- They hunt fish, crabs, lobsters and even octopuses.

Sharks don't just swim and hunt. Some like to have a rest. **WHITE-TIPPED REEF SHARKS** sleep by day in caves or under rocks. They often rub their backs against the rocks to get rid of pests. But at night, they go their separate ways and swim off to hunt.

The white-tipped fins make this shark easy to recognize.

These sharks may be still by day, but if a tasty fish comes near – they wake up in a flash!

Close eyes!

When a shark attacks, a special piece of skin called a membrane slides down to protect its eyes.

This big fin, on the side of the body near the front, is a shark's pectoral fin.

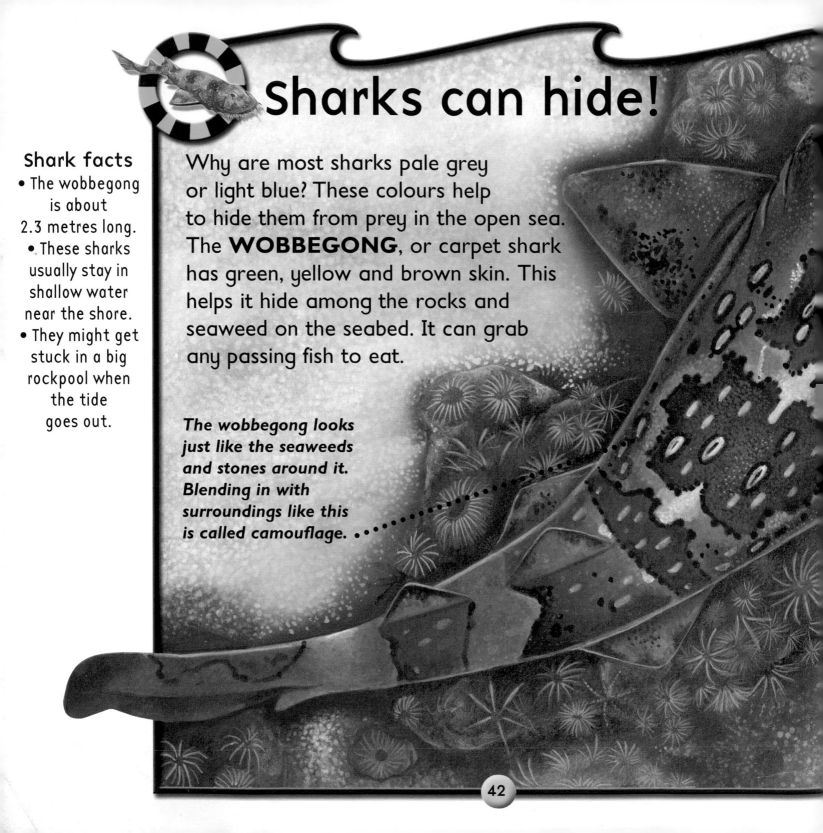

Sharks can hide!

Shark facts

- The wobbegong is about 2.3 metres long.
- These sharks usually stay in shallow water near the shore.
- They might get stuck in a big rockpool when the tide goes out.

Why are most sharks pale grey or light blue? These colours help to hide them from prey in the open sea. The **WOBBEGONG**, or carpet shark has green, yellow and brown skin. This helps it hide among the rocks and seaweed on the seabed. It can grab any passing fish to eat.

The wobbegong looks just like the seaweeds and stones around it. Blending in with surroundings like this is called camouflage.

Carpet shark!

Find a carpet with plenty of colours. Get some patches of paper the same colours. Sticky-tape them onto some old clothes and lie on the carpet. Are you well camouflaged, like the wobbegong?

The wobbegong lies very still on the seabed waiting for a meal. It may not move for hours!

A bendy skeleton

Shark facts
- The megamouth is 4.5 metres long.
- It weighs about one tonne.
- Megamouths live in deep water where it is very dark.

The **MEGAMOUTH** is a mysterious shark of the deep ocean. Like other sharks, it has no bones! Every shark has a strong skeleton inside its body, with parts like a skull and ribs. But these parts are not made of bone. They are made of rubbery, bendy material called cartilage.

New discovery!

No one had ever seen a megamouth until 1976, when one was caught near Hawaii in the Pacific Ocean.

The megamouth does not chase after prey, like most other sharks. It swims along slowly.

The megamouth's mouth really is mega! It's about one metre across – and it glows in the dark! But the teeth are tiny.

Like whale sharks and basking sharks, megamouths suck in tiny animals such as krill and baby fish.

The loose skin and floppy fins show that the megamouth is a slow swimmer.

Deadly sharks!

Shark facts

- Tiger sharks reach more than six metres in length.
- They are wide and bulky too, so they can weigh more than 1.5 tonnes.
- Some people who were thought to be eaten by great whites, were probably attacked by tiger sharks.

Some sharks have huge appetites and will eat almost anything. The **TIGER SHARK** eats fish, seals, turtles, dolphins, sea birds, squid, crabs, other sharks, and almost anything else. Tiger sharks have also been known to swim along the coast and attack people in water that's only waist-deep.

In a shark, new teeth are always growing to replace the ones which wear out or snap off. So the tiger shark is always ready to bite!

The tiger shark is big and powerful. It could swallow this monk seal in one gulp.

46

Tiger sharks are born with stripes on their sides. These fade as the shark gets older.

Dustbin shark!

Tiger sharks have swallowed leftover food thrown from ships, also tin cans, lumps of wood, training shoes, and even a tom-tom — a type of drum!

Tiger sharks can be big and heavy. Some can even rival great whites in size.

Mantises are preying

Bug facts
• Mantises live in warmer parts of the world, especially tropical forests.
• The biggest have a total body length of 15 centimetres.

Many bugs are predators, or hunters. Few insects are fiercer than the **PRAYING MANTIS**. It is named because its front legs are folded, as if praying. But really, it is preying. It watches a fly or moth come near, then SNAP. It snatches the victim with a grab too fast for us to see.

The mantis usually walks slowly using its back four legs. But it can open its wings and fly, to escape enemies or attract a mate.

48

The mantis has massive eyes and hunts mainly by sight Sometimes it may creep up on prey, but usually it snatches the meal out of mid air.

The mantis's green colour blends with the leaves around it. Even its eyes match! Its prey does not notice any danger until it is too late.

The front legs fold back on themselves to stick their sharp spines into a victim. The mantis's 'jaws' move from side to side. They chop and tear up the meal, usually starting with the head!

Mantis wings!

Most insects have wings. They are usually folded over the back, but are used to fly the insect from danger.

Bees do not mind dying

Bug facts
• A big honey bee nest has more than 50,000 worker bees, who are all sisters.
• Only one, the queen bee, lays eggs. She is larger than all the others.

HONEY BEES are social insects. This means they live in a group, or colony, in a nest. They share jobs such as finding food, cleaning the nest and caring for the young. In fact, they will even die for each other so that the whole colony can survive.

Some bees forage outside, searching for sweet flower nectar. Then they return to the nest and 'dance' to tell other bees where the flowers are.

Flower power!

As bees collect pollen, they spread it from flower to flower, to make new seeds. With fewer bees, there would be fewer flowers.

The bee's sting is at its rear end. If it jabs the sting into an enemy, the back part of its body is torn off, and the bee is certain to die.

A nest has hundreds of six-sided cells with wax walls. Here, young bees hatch into grubs.

Some cells contain stored food the bees have made from nectar and pollen – this is honey.

Monarchs fly long-distance!

No insect flies farther than a **MONARCH BUTTERFLY**. Each year these big butterflies fly hundreds of kilometres on their long journeys, called migrations.

The monarch's wings are 10 centimetres across. The bright patterns and the spots on the body warn enemies that this butterfly tastes horrible!

Bug facts
• After a winter rest, monarchs fly north in the spring – they stop to breed, then they die.
• Monarchs are also called milkweed butterflies, as their caterpillars feed only on this plant.
• Monarch caterpillars are about 5 centimetres in length.

Full circle
Butterflies lay eggs, which hatch into caterpillars, which become chrysalises, which ... become butterflies!

Each wing is covered with thousands of tiny, coloured, flakelike scales.

The butterfly senses wind and air currents with its long antennae (feelers). These also 'smell' the air for scents of flowers.

Monarchs can fly an amazing 2000 kilometres on migration, covering 150 kilometres in a single day!

The two wings on each side are joined by a tiny hook. This allows both the front and back wings to flap as one.

The monarch's 'tongue' is shaped like a coiled-up drinking straw. It unrolls to sip the flower's juices and nectar.

Locusts love leaves!

Bug facts
- The biggest locust swarms have measured more than 50 kilometres in length.
- They contained more than 250 billion locusts.

Desert **LOCUSTS** are a type of grasshopper. They live in dry, remote areas. But sometimes, when rains come and plants grow quickly, locusts feed well and breed well. Then they feed more and breed more. Soon there are millions of them, and they take to the air in a huge, hungry cloud.

Locusts live in all warm places. The biggest swarms are found in Africa.

54

A giant swarm of locusts darkens the sky for hours as it flies in search of food.

If locusts find a field of crops, they swoop down and begin to feast. The whole field can be gone in less than an hour.

As locusts feed, they crawl or hop from plant to plant. They use their long, strong back legs to leap away from danger.

In one day, a single locust can fly 20 kilometres and then eat its own weight in food — mainly plant leaves, stems, shoots and buds.

Hopping mad!

When locusts hatch, they are wingless hoppers. They have to jump between meals.

Beetles can be kings

Bug facts
• The great diving beetle grows to 5 centimetres in length.
• Various kinds of diving beetles live in ponds all over the world.

A pond is like a mini-jungle, where the **GREAT DIVING BEETLE** is king of the hunters. It is fast and fierce, with large, fanglike jaws to seize and stab victims such as tadpoles, worms and baby fish. No small creature is safe from this thumb-sized underwater terror!

The beetle hunts using its big eyes. Its antennae (feelers) detect ripples in the water caused by escaping prey.

The victim is grabbed by pincer-like feet on the beetle's front legs, then pulled towards its long, sharp jaws.

The great diving beetle comes to the surface to trap bubbles of air under the wing-cases on its back. It breathes this stored air while underwater.

This is a female great diving beetle – she has grooves, or furrows, along the wing-cases on her back. The male's back is smooth and shiny.

The bristly legs work like paddles to row through the water.

A tasty meal

Diving beetles quickly catch prey that fall into the pond – from flies to worms.

Army ants march on

Bug facts
- Some colonies of army ants in South America have more than one million 'soldiers'.
- Similar ants, called driver ants, live in African forests.

ARMY ANTS march in long lines across the tropical forest floor, left right three times (with their six legs), until they feel hungry. Then they stop. Some gather round to set up a simple nest for a few days. Others set out to find food — and kill any creature they find.

The ants crowd around a victim, bite and sting it, then chop it into tiny pieces with their strong 'jaws'.

Pieces of food are taken back to the rest of the colony, in the nest.

58

Any animal that cannot escape is attacked by the ants. They can strip the meat off a wild pig in four hours. Even the giant anteater runs away from army ants!

Giant queen

Only a queen ant lays eggs. She is huge, five times bigger than a guard, which is twice as big as a worker.

Small groups called scouting parties search for more food.

Moths like moonlight

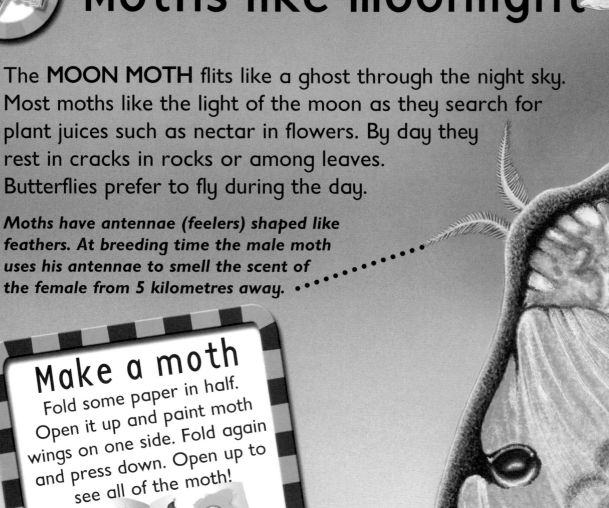

Bug facts
• Moon moths are large, with wings 15 centimetres across.
• Atlas moths are even bigger – with wings almost 30 centimetres across they are the largest flying insects.

The **MOON MOTH** flits like a ghost through the night sky. Most moths like the light of the moon as they search for plant juices such as nectar in flowers. By day they rest in cracks in rocks or among leaves. Butterflies prefer to fly during the day.

Moths have antennae (feelers) shaped like feathers. At breeding time the male moth uses his antennae to smell the scent of the female from 5 kilometres away.

Make a moth
Fold some paper in half. Open it up and paint moth wings on one side. Fold again and press down. Open up to see all of the moth!

60

The moon moth's long 'tails' are mainly for show, to attract a partner. The two 'dance' in the moonlight. By day, as the moth rests, the tails look like old, curled-up leaves.

The wide wings have large spots, like staring eyes. At a quick glance, this makes the moth look like a big-eyed owl, which scares away enemies.

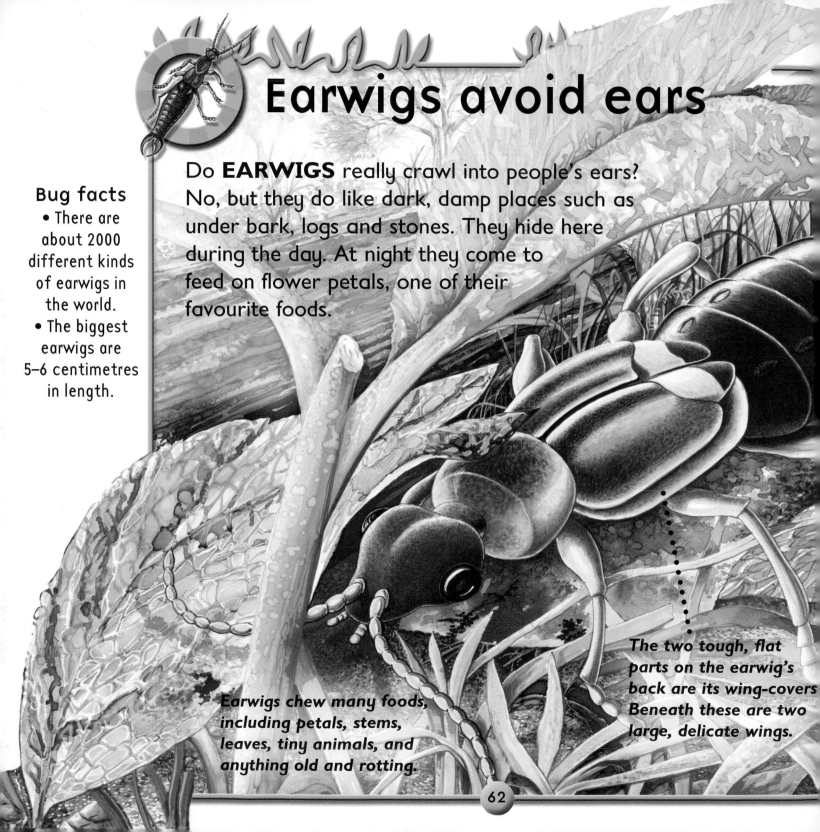

Earwigs avoid ears

Do **EARWIGS** really crawl into people's ears? No, but they do like dark, damp places such as under bark, logs and stones. They hide here during the day. At night they come to feed on flower petals, one of their favourite foods.

Bug facts
• There are about 2000 different kinds of earwigs in the world.
• The biggest earwigs are 5–6 centimetres in length.

Earwigs chew many foods, including petals, stems, leaves, tiny animals, and anything old and rotting.

The two tough, flat parts on the earwig's back are its wing-covers Beneath these are two large, delicate wings.

The tail pincers are used to fold up the wings after flying. The earwig also holds its partner by the tail pincers when breeding.

The female earwig has almost straight pincers. The male's are more curved, like a C.

Earwigs have a low, flat body. They can crawl into a narrow opening to hide from enemies, such as spiders, frogs and birds.

Mother-wig

A mother earwig takes good care of her eggs. She cleans and protects them.

Dragonflies have bug-eyes!

Bug facts
• In ancient times, before dinosaurs, lived huge dragonflies with wings 60 centimetres across.

• Today's dragonflies are smaller. But they are still big for insects, with wingspans of up to 20 centimetres.

DRAGONFLIES have huge eyes. They take up over half the head. Expert hunters, dragonflies have a sharp mouth for cutting up their meals.

Water baby
A young dragonfly, called a nymph, lacks wings and it lives in a pond! But it is just as fierce at hunting as its parents.

The wings make a whirring noise as they beat up and down ten times every second.

This is a hawker dragonfly. It has a long, slim body and swoops to and fro over the same area near a pond or river.

Darter dragonflies have shorter, fatter bodies. They sit on a perch and dart out when they spot a meal flying by.

When it has found a meal, the dragonfly returns to its perch. There it begins to bite the victim into pieces, to eat the softer parts.

The dragonfly's eye is made of many tiny parts. Each one sees a small area of the view. A dragonfly has more of these parts than any other bug, more than 30,000 in each eye!

The ground under the dragonfly's perch is covered with legs, wings and other bits from its meal that were too tough to eat.

Dragonflies catch their food with their legs. They hold out the front legs like a 'basket' to scoop up flies, gnats and moths.

Bugs can bring death

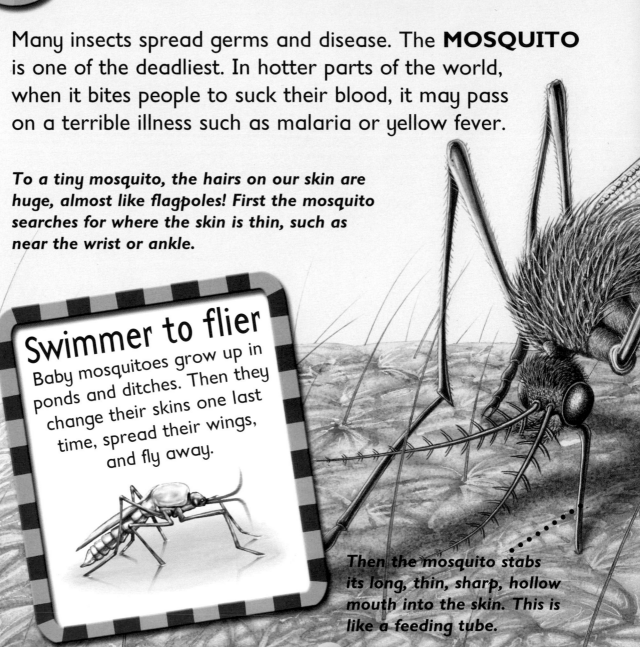

Bug facts

- The disease malaria is spread by a type of mosquito called the anopheles. It kills nearly 3 million people each year.
- Other diseases spread by flies, fleas, lice and other bugs kill more than 50 million people each year.

Many insects spread germs and disease. The **MOSQUITO** is one of the deadliest. In hotter parts of the world, when it bites people to suck their blood, it may pass on a terrible illness such as malaria or yellow fever.

To a tiny mosquito, the hairs on our skin are huge, almost like flagpoles! First the mosquito searches for where the skin is thin, such as near the wrist or ankle.

Swimmer to flier

Baby mosquitoes grow up in ponds and ditches. Then they change their skins one last time, spread their wings, and fly away.

Then the mosquito stabs its long, thin, sharp, hollow mouth into the skin. This is like a feeding tube.

Next the mosquito sucks up blood through its tubelike mouth.

As the mosquito sucks, its body swells up like a warm, red balloon. Then the mosquito slides out its feeding tube and buzzes off, before the person realizes what has happened.

It is usually female mosquitoes that feed on blood. They use its nutrients to make their eggs. Most male mosquitoes are not blood-suckers. They feed on flowers, plants and moulds.

Fierce spiders

Spider facts
• The Sydney funnelweb lives in Eastern Australia.
• Its head and body are 4 to 5 centimetres long.
• It can live for more than five years.

Some spiders are very shy. If you go too near, they hide in a dark corner. The **FUNNELWEB SPIDER** of Australia may do this – or it may rear up, show its big fangs, and get ready to strike. This is very dangerous. The funnelweb is a big, strong spider, and its bite can kill a person.

Prey get trapped by the outer silk threads and the spider poisons them with its bite.

68

The funnelweb feeds at night on insects trapped by its silk threads. It feels for its food in the dark with its long front legs.

Spider danger!

Where poisonous spiders live, never put your hands into holes or corners. Use a stick to lift rocks or plants. Wear gloves and boots.

The threads make a funnel shape that leads to the spider's lair – a hole under a rock or root.

Wonderful webs

Spider facts
- Orb-web spiders live all over the world, especially in woods and hedges.
- They are usually 1 to 3 centimetres in length.

All spiders can make silk threads, but not all spiders make webs from them. The **ORB-WEB SPIDER** weaves a beautiful web shaped like a wheel. It has strong, straight threads, which look like the spokes on a wheel, and sticky spiral threads to catch the spider's prey.

Long, straight threads give the web strength.

New from old!

The orb-web spider makes a new web each day. First, it eats the old one, to recycle it. This means less new silk has to be made.

Spiral threads are soft, stretchy and sticky. Flies and moths just can't escape from them.

The whole web takes about one hour to build.

70

If the spider has just eaten, it will wrap up any new prey in silk threads, and store it at the web's edge. This is a snack for later on!

The spider waits in the middle of the web. When a victim gets caught and struggles, the spider feels the threads pull with its feet. It follows the tugs to find its meal.

Spiders can swim!

Spider facts

- The water spider lives in ponds, lakes and ditches in Europe and parts of Asia.
- Its head and body are 1.5 centimetres in length.

Few spiders live in water. In fact, there's only one! The **WATER SPIDER** breathes air like other spiders. By bringing small air bubbles under the water, this spider uses them to make a bigger bubble. This bubble home provides the spider with air.

The big bubble or 'air bell' is the water spider's home. It stays inside most of the time. It eats, rests, and even breeds there.

The spider spins a dome of silk threads tied to water plants and pebbles. These trap the big bubble of air.

The spider visits the surface to gather air. It traps small air bubbles between its legs and in its body hairs. It carries them underwater to add to the big bubble.

The spider pokes its legs out of the bubble to see if it can catch tadpoles, insects and tiny fish. It dashes out to bite them, and brings them back to eat.

Sea spider

The sea spider looks like a spider and lives in the sea. But it is not a real spider, just a close cousin.

Spiders can be deadly

Spider facts

- Black widows live in warm parts of the world.
- They are found in many habitats, from grasslands to gardens.
- The head and body are 1.3 centimetres in length.

All spiders have a poisonous bite, to kill prey or stop it struggling. But only a few spiders have poison powerful enough to harm a person. One which does is the **BLACK WIDOW**. It is small, shiny and black, and its bite can kill a human. So can its close cousin, the redback spider.

New for old!

All spiders grow by casting off, or moulting, their 'skin' — the old body case. There's a new, bigger one underneath.

The female black widow is usually the one which harms people. If she feels threatened, she tries to hide or run away. But sometimes she has to bite in self defence.

After mating the female may eat the male! This is why she is called the black 'widow'. She no longer has a partner.

The female black widow is larger than the male. She has a red mark shaped like an '8' on the underside of her body.

Big, hairy spiders

Spider facts
- Big, hairy tarantulas and bird-eating spiders live in tropical places.
- The head and body are up to 12 centimetres in length.
- The legs measure more than 25 centimetres across.

The biggest spiders in the world are hairy and huge – bigger than your hand. These **TARANTULAS** or bird-eating spiders really do eat birds, especially baby birds in nests. They also hunt insects, worms, and even lizards, mice and baby rats!

This female tarantula is guarding her eggs. They are surrounded by a shell, or cocoon, of silk. When the babies hatch, they look like tiny versions of their mother.

As dusk falls, the tarantula sets off to hunt. Most types prowl around on the ground, but some actually live in trees.

Spider hands!
Put on an old pair of gloves and stick two buttons to the thumbs. Link your thumbs together and walk like a tarantula!

Tarantulas have huge fangs which can bite very hard. But most are not especially poisonous. They rely on their strength and size.

Some spiders spit!

Spider facts
• Spitting spiders grow to 1.2 centimetres.
• They live in all regions except Australia and New Zealand.

SPITTING SPIDERS don't spit ordinary spit. They squirt a sticky liquid, like glue, from their fangs. This sprays over their prey like a rope or net. The prey gets tangled up and stuck down. Then the spitting spider moves in, delivers its poison bite, and begins to feed.

The spitting spider has only six eyes, not eight like other spiders.

Spitting spiders catch tiny insects such as ants, flies, gnats and midges.

The spit becomes thick and sticky as soon as it comes out of the spider's fangs.

Spitting spiders often hunt on fences and walls around houses.

The spider shakes its head from side to side as it sprays. So the spit forms two wavy, zig-zag ropes that fall onto the victim and pin it down.

Spitting distance

The spitting spider can spit three times its own length!

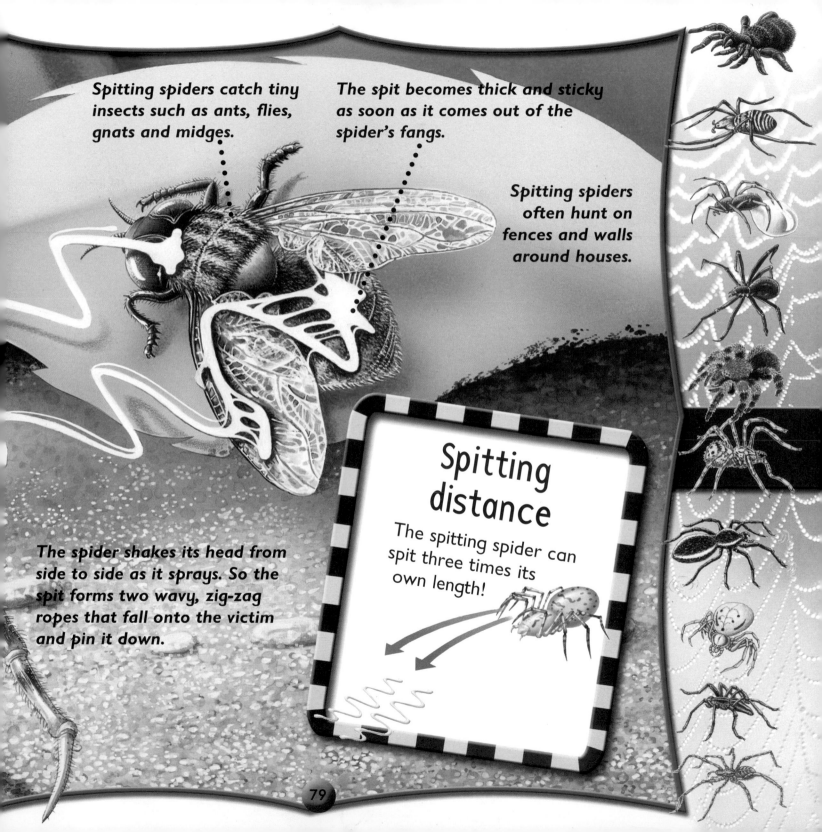

Walking on water

Spider facts

- Raft spiders live in marshes, swamps and ponds around the world.
- Most are large, with a head and body up to 4 centimetres long.

The **RAFT SPIDER** sits on a leaf or stone, at the edge of a pond or marsh. Its front legs dip in the water and detect the tiny ripples of small creatures moving nearby. The spider dashes across the water, grabs its victim, and races back to land to eat its meal.

Raft spiders are big enough to grab young fish, water insects, pond snails, tadpoles and even small frogs.

The raft spider feels for its prey with its front legs and also with its palps – these look like short legs on either side of the fangs.

The spider's hairy body, legs and feet trap tiny bubbles of air. These stop the spider sinking under the water's surface.

Fishing for flies!

Fish for flies using a magnet, string and paper clips with paper 'wings'. The 'flies' stick to the magnet if you're quick enough!

Wearing disguises

Spider facts
- Crab spiders live in most parts of the world, especially grasslands and forests.
- The head and body are about 1 centimetre in length.

It's not the flower that kills — it's the **CRAB SPIDER** hiding there. This spider is coloured and shaped to look like part of the flower. Blending into the surroundings like this is called camouflage. Many spiders do it. They look like leaves, bark, twigs and even bird droppings!

Crab spiders have wide bodies, and they walk sideways too — just like real crabs at the seaside.

Many little creatures visit flowers, such as bees, flies, beetles and ants. The crab spider eats them all! It has strong poison for its size. It surprises the visitor with a sudden bite which quickly causes death.

Crabs of many colours!

Crab spiders come in many colours, from white, yellow and pink, to red, green and grey. They always sit in a flower of the same colour.

The crab spider keeps very still, until the victim is close enough to bite.

Speedy hunter

Spider facts
- Wolf spiders live in most regions, among leaves and grass.
- The head and body are about 1–2 centimetres in length.

The **WOLF SPIDER** does not weave a web. It is a hunter and chases after victims, like a tiny version of a real wolf. It uses its eight big eyes to see, and its eight long legs to run fast.

The wolf spider hunts mainly by sight. Its very large eyes point forwards, for a good view of its prey.

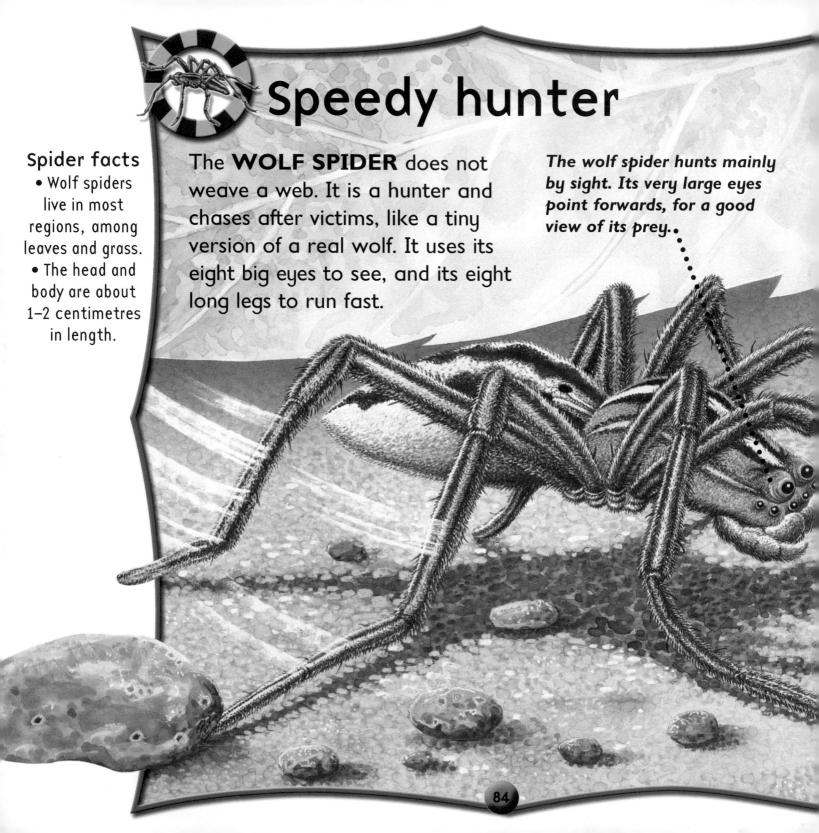

84

All spiders have a large head, with eight legs attached, and a rounded body. The wolf spider's head and body are small, but its legs are very long and strong.

Wolf spiders sunbathe on pebbles, soil or leaves before they hunt.

The wolf spider eats any creature it can catch, from a slow slug to a leaping cricket..

Making babies!

The female wolf spider lays eggs and wraps them all in a silk case for protection. A few weeks later, the baby spiders hatch.

Spiders hate baths!

Spider facts
• House spiders live in outbuildings, homes and sheds.
• The head and body are up to 2 centimetres in length.

HOUSE SPIDERS don't go in the bath to get clean. They prowl about at night, go too near the edge of a bath or sink, and slide in by accident. They can't climb back out because the walls are too steep and slippery. They need help!

The palps feel the way.

The fangs seize and bite prey.

Save a spider!

Put a glass over the spider, slide card under it and lift the card and glass together. Put the spider outside. If you can't do this – ask someone who can!

House spiders are helpful. They eat flies, mosquitoes and other pests. If there's one in the bath or sink – save it!

House spiders spin untidy-looking webs in corners. The sheet-like web is triangle-shaped. It's called a cobweb.

Barn owls live nearly everywhere

BARN OWLS do not just live in barns. They rest and nest in church towers, old buildings, hollow trees and caves in cliffs. Also they live in many different places, from cold mountains to tropical forests.

The barn owl is one of the most widespread birds. It is found in the far north, the far south – and everywhere between!

Owl facts
• The barn owl is about 35 centimetres long, from beak to tail-tip.
• It lays more eggs than any other owl – in some years there can be more than ten.

Too bright
Barn owls swoop on animals injured by cars on roads – then get blinded by headlights and cannot see to fly away.

Barn owls catch a huge range of prey, from mice, rats and voles, to baby birds, lizards, grubs, beetles and worms.

The barn owl is snow-white underneath, and looks ghostly in the moonlight.

The owl swoops out of the darkness in deathly silence. It holds its wings still, and its soft-edged feathers make no sound.

The barn owl's feet have strong toes and long claws called talons. These jab into the prey and hold it with a powerful grip.

Owls fly by day!

Owl facts
• The snowy is one of the largest owls, measuring up to 70 centimetres from beak to tail-tip.
• It is the biggest hunting bird of the Arctic region.

Most owls fly secretly at night. But the **SNOWY OWL** of the far north flies in daylight too. It has no choice. During the short summer, its Arctic home is the 'land of the midnight sun'. There is no darkness at all!

The snowy owl cannot nest in trees as there are none on the rocky, grassy northern lands called the Arctic tundra.

A hunting owl flies slowly and silently, wing-tip feathers spread and body swaying. Its head is held steady, looking and listening for prey.

Snowy owls nest in a hollow among stones and moss. The female lays up to ten eggs over three to four weeks. If prey is scarce, she lays just one. She tears up the meaty meals for her chicks.

Snowy owls catch lemmings, mice, voles, rats, rabbits, and many kinds of small birds. The male brings food to the nest.

Whoo's whoo?

In most owls, female and male look similar. The male snowy has fewer dark flecks than the female — he is almost pure white.

Owls go fishing

Many owls hunt over land. **FISH OWLS** fly over rivers and lakes in the moonlight. They look and listen for ripples and bubbles, which are signs of fish or similar creatures just under the water. To catch their prey, fish owls do not mind getting their feet wet!

Owl facts
• There are seven kinds of fish owl across Africa, South Asia and East Asia.
• Blakiston's fish owl of China and Japan is huge, with wings nearly 2 metres across.

Wading in water
Owls do not always swoop from the air. The fish owl may go paddling in shallow water, using its feet to help it find food.

Fish owls have legs, toes and claws that are all extra-long. Their legs are mostly bare, because feathers would get wet and heavy.

Fish owls eat more than fish. They grab lizards, frogs, freshwater crabs and crayfish, small waterbirds, water-rats and water-voles. They even take young rabbits that come to the water's edge for a drink.

The fish owl skims over the surface, aiming towards the bubbles and ripples. It then flicks out its long legs to grab its slippery supper from just under the water.

The owl's toes are covered with tiny scales. They help its long, sharp talons (claws) to grip the smooth, scaly, wriggly fish.

Owls go to church

Owl facts
- The little owl is not the smallest owl, but it is little – about 20 centimetres from beak to tail-tip.
- It lives across the whole of Asia, from Spain to China, and also in North Africa.

LITTLE OWLS also go to temples, shrines and mosques. They like the tall towers and quiet surroundings. By day they roost (rest) and at night they hunt in parks, gardens and fields.

Little owls often come out just before dusk. They are more likely to be seen by people than owls that fly at night.

Small and short

The well-named little owl is quite a bit smaller than a pigeon, or even a blackbird, although like most owls, its tail is short.

Since ancient times, little owls have lived in towns and cities. Swooping from a church or temple, they were seen as symbols of wisdom and good luck.

The little owl's loud calls carry a long way in the still of the evening. They include 'kee-uuw', like a loud cat's miaow, and 'wheere-ooww', similar to a dog's yelp.

In the countryside, little owls prefer old trees such as oaks, willows and palms. They like the holes that form where branches have broken.

Little owls hunt little prey – worms, beetles, slugs and spiders. A mouse or sparrow is a huge feast for the little owl!

Owls have no horns!

Owl facts

• The great horned owl is widespread in North and South America, in forests, woods, parks, scrub and desert.

• It is about 50 centimetres from beak to tail-tip.

The **GREAT HORNED OWL** has tufts of feathers on its head. They look like horns, or ears. But an owl's real ears are hidden by its plumage (feathers). An owl can hear as well as it can see — or even better!

The ears of the great horned owl are on the sides of its head, at about the same level as the eyes.

What big eyes!

Make an owl head as big as a human one, with a face mask from card. See how huge the eyes are — bigger than yours!

The deep hooting of the male means: 'Other owls stay away.' He makes four deep hoots, 'boo-whoo-whoo-whoo'.

At breeding time, a nearby female great horned owl answers back. She makes about seven hoots that are even deeper!

Then the two get together and make yet more strange noises which sound like cats purring, babies crying and people laughing.

The owl's powerful hooked bill (beak) tears up mice, rats, rabbits, gophers, prairie dogs, and even squirrels and small monkeys.

Some owls have lots of names

Owl facts

• The boobook owl lives in Southeast Asia, south-eastern Australia and New Zealand.

• Its many noises include a squeal like cats fighting.

The **BOOBOOK OWL** is named after its 'booo-book' call. It is also called the morepork or mopoke owl, after its other calls. And the cat owl, too – it can miaow!

Boobook owls are common in some areas, and do not mind living around villages and towns. In early evening they even perch in the open, on a street light or telephone pole – or on a branch in a garden.

Boobooks eat mainly insects, such as cockchafer beetles and moths, which swarm around street lights. They also catch small birds, mice and baby rats.

The male and female owls call softly to each other as they get ready for the night's hunting. When they have chicks, they need to find food by day as well.

Mobbed!

If small birds find a resting owl, they 'mob' it by flapping and squawking to drive it away. After all, when darkness falls, it might eat them!

Many owls are tawny

Owl facts
- The tawny owl lives in all kinds of woodlands and forests across Europe and Asia.
- It is about 40 centimetres long from beak to tail-tip.

Tawny is a colour – a sort of orange-reddish brown. Many owls are tawny, but only one is called the **TAWNY OWL**. In the breeding season, the male calls as he returns with food for the female and chicks.

Tawny owls like plenty of trees but they can also live in towns and farmland. A female and male stay together for many years. They raise their family in the same area, or territory, year after year.

Too fluffy to fly

Owl chicks have soft, fluffy feathers to keep them warm. They grow stronger feathers when they are ready to fly.

Tawny owls like to nest in a tree hole. But they might also use a hollow among the roots, or even the old nest of a magpie or squirrel.

There are usually three eggs, which hatch after four weeks. The chicks are ready to fly off on their own when they are about five weeks old.

Owls can screech!

Which night creatures screech loudly? **SCOPS OWLS** do, time after time, calling 'chiup' every few seconds, on and on, and on and on. They keep people awake at night! This is why they are also known as screech-owls. Even though they make so much noise, they are very difficult to see!

Owl facts
- There are about 40 kinds of Scops owl, living in all regions apart from Australia.
- Most are small, the size of a human hand.

Owls roost (sleep) during the day. But their feathers blend so well into the background of tree trunks, branches and twigs, it is almost impossible to spot them. Merging with the background like this is called camouflage.

When a Scops owl is out in the open, it stays perfectly still, so it is hardly noticed. It watches for danger through narrowed eye-slits.

Owl pellets

An owl cannot digest hard bones, claws and beaks in its food. So it coughs up these bits, all pressed together into a lump called a pellet.

Like other 'eared' owls, the tufts on top of the Scops owl's head are not real ears, but long feathers.

Like most birds, an owl moults – grows new feathers as the old ones fall out, usually twice each year. Moulting is a risky time because the owl cannot fly well until its new plumage is complete.

Owls like spikes

Owl facts
• Sometimes the elf owl owl flies near campfires of people, chasing insects attracted by the light.
• It is about 14 centimetres from beak to tail-tip.

The **ELF OWL** is one of the tiniest owls. It could easily sit in your hand (if it was tame). But even though it is so small, it has little to fear when at home. Its nest hole is in a tree-sized cactus called the giant saguaro. It is one of the prickliest places in the world.

The giant saguaro is a very tall plant. The elf owl's nest hole might be 10 metres above the ground. •••••••••••••

Fierce food!
An owl's meals often fight back when caught! Worms wriggle, beetles and crickets kick and spiders bite.

The elf owl is usually too small to hunt mice. Its main meals are moths, grubs, caterpillars, crickets, beetles, centipedes, spiders and worms. It grabs many of these from the ground.

The female elf owl lays about three tiny eggs, hardly larger than grapes.

Both female and male incubate the eggs (sit on them to keep them warm) for two weeks until they hatch.

In their homeland of southwestern North America, elf owls do not just live in cactus deserts. They are also found in bushy areas and woods, especially along steep valleys and cliffs.

Owls kill owls!

Owl facts

• The eagle owl is probably the biggest owl, about 70 centimetres from beak to tail-tip.

• It is found across most of Europe, North Africa and Asia – but it is getting more scarce.

The **EAGLE OWL** is so big and strong that it hunts other hunters. It may catch another owl, like a tawny, or a bird of prey like a buzzard or goshawk, sleeping on a branch.

Eagle versus owl

An eagle owl can weigh as much as an eagle, although it has a bigger head and shorter tail.

Eagle owls can hunt large prey and have been known to attack small deer and even foxes.

The eagle owl is found mainly in high mountains and rocky, dry scrubland. Even real eagles keep away from this powerful predator.

106

Ear tufts on the eagle owl's head have nothing to do with its hearing. It is thought they may help to camouflage (hide) the owl in its surroundings.

The eagle owl's massive claws stab into its prey like curved nails. There is no escape for the victim.

Woodland is being cut down where these owls like to nest. The eagle owl is becoming scarce because of this.

Babies climb trees

Orang facts
• There are two kinds of orangs found in Borneo and Sumatra, Southeast Asia.
• They are very rare, and are protected by law.
• 'Orang-utan' means 'mystery man of the woods'.

A baby **ORANG-UTAN** is like a baby human, except hairier! It sleeps a lot, cries when hungry or frightened, and goes to the toilet where it wants. But the mother orang is very caring and protects her baby from enemies – including huge eagles!

As the young orang grows, it begins to try different foods. It will eat mainly fruits, also flowers and buds, with the odd snack of a juicy lizard or bird's egg.

Orangs usually live alone, except for a mother and baby. They may stay together for as long as eight years.

Orang-utans live in trees all their lives. They are expert climbers because they have four 'hands' – their feet and toes grasp almost as well as their hands and fingers.

Like all baby mammals, the young orang feeds on its mother's milk. But, compared to other mammals, it does this for a very long time – three years or more!

Bend a branch!
The male orang is twice as big as the female. At 80 kilograms, he is the world's heaviest tree-living creature.

A very rare baby

Panda facts
- Pandas live only in south and west China.
- There are less than 1000 left in the wild.

A newborn **GIANT PANDA** cub is not a giant. It is smaller than your hand, white all over, has almost no fur, and its eyes are tightly closed! But the cub grows quickly. By six weeks old it can leave its den and follow its mother. By six months old it is eating its life-long favourite food, bamboo.

The baby panda is born in a den, in a cave or hollow tree. The mother leaves it twice daily, for an hour or two, for food and water.

The panda appears to have a sixth finger. But this is really a long, bendy part of its wrist. It is used to hold bamboo stems and leaves.

Panda meals are very boring – bamboo, bamboo and more bamboo. But sometimes they eat fruits, eggs, insects and even the meat from a dead animal.

Hi, panda-face!

Make this famous animal face from white card, with four black circles. Can people guess what you are?

It is hard for young pandas to find somewhere to set up home. Their bamboo forests are being cut down to make way for farmland.

Chicks live on ice!

No baby grows up in a colder place than the **EMPEROR PENGUIN** chick. It is −50 degrees Celsius in icy Antarctica, colder than a food deep-freezer. Luckily the chick has its father to keep it warm.

Older chicks grow fluffy down feathers. They huddle together for extra warmth in the icy wind.

Father penguins shelter younger chicks in their belly feathers.

The penguin chick cheeps and pecks its parent's beak. This makes the parent bring up food from its stomach. The meal is smelly, half-rotted fish and lumps of slimy squid.

After two months at sea catching food such as shrimplike krill, the mother penguin returns to her baby. Now the father can go off to feed.

Who's taller?

The emperor penguin is the biggest penguin. It is 120 centimetres in height. How tall are you?

From milk to meat

Wolf facts

• Wolves live in almost all northern lands.

• A big wolf is 2 metres long, including its bushy tail, and weighs 60 kilograms.

For the first few weeks, baby **GREY WOLVES** stay inside. They are safe in their den, in a cave or burrow. Their mother feeds them on milk. Then they begin to leave the den and start to eat meat.

The mother wolf usually has three to five cubs. In rare cases she may have as many as ten!

114

The cubs nip, pounce, scramble and tumble. Their 'play' is practice for when they grow up to hunt prey.

Wolf cubs are brought their first meaty meals not only by their mother, but by their father too — and by other members of the pack.

Howlin' wolf

Wolves do not really howl at the Moon. They are telling other wolves: 'I'm here!'

Babies grow fast

Seal facts
- A newborn seal pup weighs 12 kilograms – four times more than a human baby!
- It grows faster than almost any other animal, doubling its weight in five days!

The **HARP SEAL** pup lives in the cold, white wilderness of the Arctic. This baby is surrounded by snow, ice and freezing cold sea – as well as hungry predators such as polar bears and wolves. The pup lies perfectly still, hoping its thick, white fur will keep it warm and unnoticed.

The pup's fur is yellow at birth. It soon becomes a 'whitecoat' for a few weeks. Then it grows a new, darker fur coat.

If a pup cannot find its mother, it wails and cries like a human baby.

A harp seal pup is a baby for only two weeks. Then its mother stops feeding it on milk, plunges into the sea, and is gone. The pup must learn to swim, dive and catch fish – fast!

Harp seals eat mainly fish such as herring, cod and capelin. They might try a snack of squid.

Down and down
Harp seals can dive more than 300 metres and stay underwater for half an hour!

Big baby

Elephant facts

- The African elephant is the largest land animal, weighing up to 8 tonnes.
- A big elephant eats 300 kilograms of grass and other plants daily – which is the weight of five full-grown people!

An **ELEPHANT** baby has the world's biggest, strongest family for protection – not only its mother, but also older sisters, aunties, and even grandmother, who leads the whole herd!

For the first year or two, the calf hardly strays more than a metre or two from its mother's legs.

The mother constantly touches her baby with her trunk. If she is busy feeding, an older sister or aunt 'babysits' and keeps the calf out of danger.

The baby feeds on its mother's milk for up to four years.

Cool, mum!

When a baby elephant wants to rest, its mother stands so that her shadow keeps the baby shaded and cool.

A young male elephant leaves the main herd at about 10 to 12 years of age. He teams up with other young males to form a smaller herd.

Fawns have spots

- The biggest deer mother, the moose, has the heaviest fawn. It weighs 15 kilograms.
- Only one type of female deer has antlers – the caribou or reindeer.

As the midsummer sun shines through leaves and twigs, it forms light spots on the woodland floor – just like the spots on a fawn's coat. The **FAWN** lies still and silent under a bush. Its mother is nearby, feeding and watching. She comes to her fawn for a few minutes, two or three times each day.

The doe (mother deer) visits her baby briefly, to feed it on her milk. Then she goes back to the main group, or herd.

The fawn's coat is dappled, with white spots on brown fur. It blends in with patches of sunlight on the ground, so the fawn is very difficult to see.

Big-head!
A buck is a full-grown male deer. He grows huge antlers each summer. They fall off in late winter.

The fawn has huge ears, big eyes and a keen nose to detect danger. If an enemy comes too near, the fawn jumps up and bounds away through the trees.

This fawn is a fallow deer. Female fallow deer do not have antlers. Males begin to grow them at about two years old.

The fawn stays hidden for a few weeks, visited by its mother. Then it joins the herd and begins to eat leaves.

Shy baby

Kangaroo facts

• When a joey is born, it is one of the tiniest mammal babies.

A baby kangaroo is called a **JOEY**. For the first six months its feet never touch the ground! It lives in its mother's pocket-shaped pouch and feeds on her milk. Gradually, the joey grows strong enough to leave the pouch and explore. But if danger appears, it soon hops back in again.

• At birth, it is smaller than your little finger, with no fur, and closed eyes.

A young joey is very shy. It rushes back to the pouch every minute! Soon it becomes bolder and stays out of the pouch longer.

Kangaroos live in very dry places in Australia, eating grass and leaves. They can go for days without water.

The older joey still pops its head into its mother's pouch to feed on her milk, until it is almost a year old.

The mother kangaroo has to clean her pouch often, using her hand claws, teeth and tongue. She throws out bits of dirt and fur that her joey leaves behind — and its droppings too!

When the joey is eight months old it leaves the pouch — and never comes back. But it still stays near its mother.

Hop-hop-hop

Can you hop like a kangaroo? Keep your feet together, knees bent, and hands held up like paws.

Babies love to play!

Many youngsters like to play – especially **OTTER** babies! They roll, tumble and jump in the riverbank mud. Sometimes they have pretend fights. But this 'play' is practice for when the otter babies, called kits, have to hunt their own food.

Otter facts

• Most animals have babies in spring or summer, but mother otters can give birth at any time of the year.

• The kits cannot open their eyes until they are four weeks old.

The kits stay in their burrow, called a holt, for more than two months. Their mother feeds them on her milk. When they are three months old, she leads them out to the riverbank, where they play and learn to swim.

By the time the kits are four months old they can catch their own small prey, such as fish, baby frogs and waterbird chicks.

Young otters are also called cubs or pups.

Lazy daysy

After a big meal, the otter spends a day or two lazing on a bare patch of ground, called its 'couch' or 'sofa'.

Tiny teeth and claws

Kitten facts
- All kittens have grey-blue eyes. These change to the adult colour at 12 weeks.
- A kitten has two sets of teeth. The first set grow by eight weeks, the second after 12 weeks.

A mother cat is very busy. She has to feed her **KITTENS** on her milk, keep them warm, lick them clean every day, let them clamber all over her and stop them wandering into danger. She may have ten or more babies to care for!

A kitten's eyes are closed for the first week of life. They are fully open by about three weeks.

Like a human baby, a kitten learns to crawl first. By about four weeks old it can walk. A week later it is running and jumping, but it may still fall over!

A kitten feeds on its mother's milk for about eight weeks. It begins to eat other foods at three weeks.

The kittens sniff and rub their mother often. They can recognize each other by smell, even in total darkness.

Kittens should stay with their mother until they are eight weeks old.

Popular pets

Some years ago, dogs were the most popular pets. Now cats have taken over. How many pet cats do you know?

Tigers are biggest

Cat facts
• The Siberian tiger measures 3.5 metres long, from nose to tail-tip.
• It weighs up to 300 kilograms – as much as five adult people.

The **SIBERIAN TIGER** is not just a big cat – it's the biggest cat! This huge hunter prowls the cold, snowy lands of Eastern Asia. It is the rarest kind of tiger, too, with less than 200 left in the wild. The Bengal tiger of the Indian region is more common, with about 5000 living wild.

The tiger has long fur on its cheeks, making its face look wide.

The Siberian tiger has thick fur to keep it warm in the ice and snow of winter.

Tigers have black stripes on their yellow, orange or gold fur. The Siberian tiger has more white in its coat to help it blend in with its snowy landscape.

Man-eaters!

Very rarely, tigers attack and eat people. These tigers are usually old or injured. They can't catch their normal prey such as deer, wild cattle and wild pigs.

The Siberian tiger is heavily built. Its body hangs close to the ground.

Pumas make good mothers

- The puma has a nose-to-tail length of 2.2 metres.
- It lives in western North America and South America.

Like all big cats, the female **PUMA** is a very caring mother. She protects her babies, feeds them on her milk – and keeps them warm and safe in a den.

Baby big cats are called cubs. Puma cubs have spotty coats when they are first born. These fade as they get older.

Puma cubs feed on their mother's milk for about seven weeks. Then they begin to eat pieces of meat which their mother brings back to the den.

The mother cat licks her babies clean. She often moves them to a new den for extra safety.

Useful tails

Like the puma, the domestic cat has a long tail. This helps it to balance as it walks along narrow surfaces, and as it runs.

A mother puma usually has two or three cubs, but there may be as many as six!

Lions live in groups

Cat facts
- The male lion is 3 metres long and weighs 200 kilograms.
- The female lion is 2.5 metres long and weighs 130 kilograms.

LIONS are the only kind of cat that live together in a group. All other cats live alone (except for a mother with her babies). A group of lions is called a pride. There are usually between five and ten lions in a pride. They are mostly mothers with their young, and one or two males. Most lions live in Africa, with just a few hundred in India.

In a pride, the chief male lion is the father of all the cubs. His main job is to chase away other lions, so that they cannot steal prey from the pride's area.

The lion is the only big cat where the female and male look different. The male is bigger and has long, shaggy neck fur called a mane.

Padded paws

Lions have thick, leathery pads on the underside of their paws. These help the lion to move quietly and get a good grip on slippery rocks.

Male and female lions roar loudly. This frightens off other lions which aren't in their pride.

Jaguars love water

Cat facts
- The jaguar grows up to 2.5 metres long, including its tail.
- It is a heavily built cat and weighs up to 150 kilograms.
- Jaguars live in Central and South America.

Many cats hate water and getting wet. The **JAGUAR** loves it! This big cat is sturdy and strong, with large, powerful muscles. It likes to hunt around rivers, lakes and swamps, and it can swim well. The jaguar catches water creatures such as turtles, caimans (types of crocodiles), crayfish and snakes. It even dives under the surface to chase fish!

After a swim, the jaguar cleans and combs its fur, using its rough tongue and its sharp claws.

American cat!
The jaguar is America's biggest cat. With its spotty coat, it is similar to the leopard of Africa and Asia.

Each 'spot' on the jaguar's coat is like a ring with a dark centre. The patchy pattern helps the jaguar to blend in with leaves and twigs.

The jaguar creeps slowly through water without a splash or a ripple. It surprises prey such as deer and tapirs.

Caracals can leap

Cat facts
• The caracal is about one metre long, including its tail.
• It lives in Africa and the Middle East.

All cats can jump well. But one of the best leapers, for its body size, is the **CARACAL**. It is not a very big cat, yet it can spring forwards more than four metres in one bound. It can even jump three metres in one leap – straight upwards!

The caracal is also called the desert lynx, because it likes dry areas – and because its ears have long tufts of fur like a real lynx.

The caracal eats rats, hares, birds, and baby animals such as antelopes and wild pigs. It also eats lizards and snakes.

The caracal lives in dry places such as rocky hills, grassland, scrub, and around the edges of deserts. Its gold colour makes it difficult to spot among the brown plants and sandy soil.

Champion leap!

The caracal can jump four times its own body length. See how far you can jump – as if you are practising for the long jump!

The caracal crouches down and then springs forwards using its powerful rear legs.

The lynx likes snow

Cat facts

- The lynx is about 1.2 metres long, including its short tail.
- Various kinds of lynx live in the north of Europe, Asia and North America.

The **LYNX** is at home in the snow and ice of the far north. It has very thick fur to keep it warm. Even the tips of its ears have furry tufts. Its paws are large and wide, and they have fur underneath, too. The paws work like snowshoes, to prevent the lynx sinking into soft snow, or sliding on slippery ice.

The lynx has a very short tail, less than 20 centimetres in length. A long tail might get so cold in the freezing winter, that it could suffer from frostbite.

Like many cats, the lynx searches for prey which are old, young, sick, or injured. These are easier to catch than strong, healthy prey!

Snow-paws!

Press your fingers into flour, which is soft and white, like snow. Now put a bag over your hand. See how your 'snow-paw' sinks in less.

The lynx hunts deer, wild sheep and goats, hares and birds. It may bury spare food in the snow and come back to eat it later.

The lynx's paws are wide and furry. They give a good grip on snow, ice, wet rocks and slippery tree branches.

Snow leopards have sharp claws

- The snow leopard lives in the high mountains of central Asia.
- It measures 2 metres long from nose to tail-tip.

The **SNOW LEOPARD**, like other big cats, has five toes on each front foot and four toes on each back foot. Every toe has a sharp claw! The claws grip trees and rocks when climbing, and they slash and slice prey when hunting.

The snow leopard also uses its claws to comb its fur and scratch its skin.

140

The rare and beautiful snow leopard hunts in mountain forests and crags. It catches wild goats, sheep, birds, monkeys and squirrels.

Smallest cat
The smallest kind of big cat is the clouded leopard of Southeast Asia. It lives almost all of its life in trees.

Like other cats, the snow leopard usually keeps its claws retracted. This means they are pulled back inside its pads, which are like pockets at the ends of its toes. This keeps the claws clean and sharp.

Servals have super-senses!

Cat facts
- The serval is about 1.2 metres long, but it is very slim and weighs only 15 kilograms.
- It lives around lakes and rivers in Africa.

All cats have amazing senses to help them hunt at night. The large eyes of the **SERVAL** see well in the dark. Its long, stiff whiskers help it to feel its way. The serval's big ears pick up sounds and its nose sniffs for food and danger. The serval is unusual for a cat as also hunts by day.

The serval has spots on its body, but stripes on its neck and upper legs.

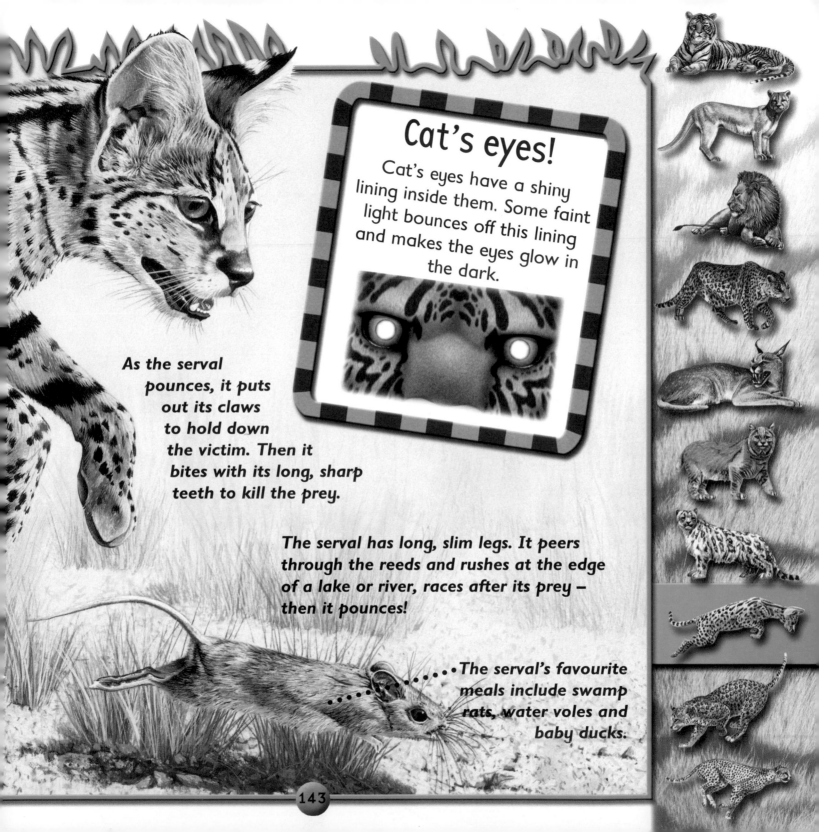

Cat's eyes!

Cat's eyes have a shiny lining inside them. Some faint light bounces off this lining and makes the eyes glow in the dark.

As the serval pounces, it puts out its claws to hold down the victim. Then it bites with its long, sharp teeth to kill the prey.

The serval has long, slim legs. It peers through the reeds and rushes at the edge of a lake or river, races after its prey — then it pounces!

The serval's favourite meals include swamp rats, water voles and baby ducks.

Leopards have a larder

Cat facts

Cat facts
• The leopard lives in many regions across Africa and southern Asia.
• It is about 2.5 metres in total length.

Sometimes a cat like the **LEOPARD** catches prey which is too big to eat in one meal. So the leopard stores the leftovers up in a tree. Here they are kept safe from hungry hyaenas and jackals too!

Leopards live in lots of places, from dry grassland and scrub to mountains, forests and swamps. They even live around villages.

The leopard may wait on a branch, and then pounce silently on a victim below.

Every leopard has a different pattern of spots – just like every person has different fingerprints.

Black leopard!

The black panther is not a different kind of big cat. It's a leopard with very dark fur.

The leopard's favourite tree has scratch marks in the bark. They warn other leopards to keep away.

The leopard is strong enough to drag a whole gazelle up into a tree.

A leopard can catch large animals such as antelopes, which are three times its own size. When food is scarce, it will eat rats, mice, birds' eggs, and even insects such as beetles!

The speedy cheetah

Cat facts
- The cheetah measures about 2 metres from nose to tail.

No animal can run as fast as the **CHEETAH**. This big cat races along at 100 kilometres per hour – almost as fast as a car on a motorway. The cheetah can only keep up this speed for half a minute. Then it must stop to cool down and get its breath back.

Cheetahs hunt small gazelles, antelopes, hares and other fast-running animals.

- It lives in Africa and western Asia.

The cheetah tries to trip or knock over its victim, then pounces on it.

Cheetahs and many other kinds of big cat have become rare. Once, cats were killed for their fur, to make coats and hats. Today, all cats need our help to survive.

The cheetah likes dry, open places such as grassland and scrub. It cannot run very fast in a thick wood!

Claws out!

The cheetah is the only cat which cannot pull its claws into its toes. The claws are big and blunt, like a dog's.

The cheetah has a small head, a slim and bendy body, and very long legs.

Bears go fishing

Bear facts

- The biggest male brown bears stand nearly 3 metres tall and weigh over 600 kilograms.
- Females are about half the size of males.
- Brown bears live in all northern lands, but mainly in remote places.

The **BROWN BEAR** rivals the polar bear as the world's biggest meat-eating land animal. It does not eat just meat. It loves fish, grubs, birds' eggs, honey from wild bees' nests, fruits, berries — in fact, just about anything. The brown bear is always hungry!

The brown bear waits for leaping salmon that swim upstream to breed. It catches them in its powerful jaws or hooks them out with its massive paws.

The brown bear enjoys feasts of fish and fruits during autumn. It puts on huge amounts of weight as layers of body fat. This is stored food to last through the long cold season.

By spring, after its long winter sleep, the bear has lost half of its body weight.

Not all brown bears are brown. Some are light grey or cream, while others are chocolate-coloured or even almost black.

Grizzled grizzly

Brown bears are called grizzlies. Their fur has white tips, making them look old, grey and 'grizzled'.

Bears go nuts!

Bear facts
- The Asian black bear is about 1.7 metres long.
- It weighs 100 to 200 kilograms.
- It lives across Asia, except for the far north and the Indian region.

Most bears eat a huge range of foods, including meat and plants. The **ASIAN BLACK BEAR** loves nuts — beechnuts, hazelnuts, walnuts, chestnuts and pinenuts. However, sometimes this bear will eat crops such as maize (sweetcorn). Then it is not the farmer's best friend.

Moon bear
The Asian black bear has a pale chest patch shaped like a V or U. This is why it is also known as the 'moon bear'.

The Asian black bear usually visits the farmer's maize fields on moonlit nights. Otherwise it prefers to live and feed in the forest.

The maize cobs are torn off by the bear's long teeth, called canines.

The Asian black bear also eats bamboo – and so does its cousin the giant panda. But the two usually avoid each other and rarely meet.

This bear can also be found in the Himalayan Mountains, where it is known as the Himalayan bear.

Some bears wear glasses!

Bear facts

- The spectacled bear is the only bear living in South America.
- It lives mainly in the forests of the Andes Mountains.
- It is up to 2 metres long and weighs 140 kilograms.

Of all the bears, the **SPECTACLED BEAR** spends most of its time in trees. It climbs by wrapping its four legs around the trunk in a 'bear hug' and then it shuffles upwards, faster than you could walk! Pale eye patches give this bear its name – spectacled. It is also called the Andean bear.

Big-eyed bear

Each spectacled bear has its own shape of eye patches. Some have small spots, others whole circles.

Like most bears, the spectacled bear lives to the age of 20 or perhaps 25 years.

Bears have long noses and an excellent sense of smell. Their hearing is also very good. But their eyes are small and they probably cannot see quite as well as we can.

Bears often stand up to look, listen and sniff for food or danger.

The spectacled bear pulls down low-growing branches so it can eat the fruits, berries or soft bark.

The spectacled bear is becoming rarer. People disturb its natural home as they take over wild areas for farmland or leisure.

Baby bears are tiny

Bear facts
- The American black bear lives in many places in North America, from frozen Alaska to hot Mexico.
- It is up to 2 metres long and weighs 300 kilograms.

A mother bear is huge, but her new babies, or cubs, are tiny. When the newborn cubs of the **AMERICAN BLACK BEAR** are curled up asleep, each is hardly bigger than your fist. Their eyes are closed, they cannot hear and they have little fur. But they grow fast. Soon the cubs can crawl about and squeak inside their safe den. When they get bigger, it is time to go outside.

The cubs are born in winter. Their den is in a cave or among the roots of a tree. The mother lines it with grass and leaves, so it is warm and comfortable.

Bear legs!
Make a walking bear from pieces of card, fixed with split-pins so the legs move. Can it walk and wave at the same time?

By watching their mother, the cubs learn how to find food and discover what is good to eat.

The cubs stay near their mother for the first year of their lives. She protects them from danger such as wolves and eagles.

Bears love honey

Bear facts

• The sun bear is about 1.2 metres long and weighs 50 kilograms.
• It lives mainly in the forests of Southeast Asia.

The **SUN BEAR** is the smallest kind of bear. It is about the size of a big dog, but much more powerful, with strong muscles, dangerous teeth and long claws. It also has the shortest fur of any bear. This bear loves honey so much, that it is sometimes called the 'honey bear'.

Long tongue

The sun bear's tongue stretches out 25 centimetres to lick food out of cracks. How long is your tongue?

All bears can climb well, but some of the bigger kinds are too heavy. The sun bear is lighter and spends much of its time in the branches.

This bear's fur varies from black to grey or rusty-brown. The rounded patch on its chest is orange or yellow – like the rising sun.

The bear tears open a bees' nest with its claws, scoops out the honeycomb with its paws and quickly licks up the honey.

Most bears have tails – but only just. The tail is very small and is often hidden in the fur of the rear end. It is not much use, except for sitting on!

Some bears snore

Bear facts
- The Eurasian brown bear is massive, but not quite as big as other brown bears such as the Kodiak bear (see page 20).
- Some live as far south as the hot lands of the Middle East.

The **EURASIAN BROWN BEAR** is a type of brown bear that lives across Europe and Asia. In the far north, where winters are long and cold, it sleeps for weeks on end. In warmer southern parts it sleeps much less.

The winter den is in a favourite rocky cave, or a large hole in a bank or under a log. The bear may sleep on and off for up to six months!

Big-foot
Bears leave tracks in snow, sand and mud. They are huge, each with a rounded paw and five long claws.

The sleeping bear curls up to keep warm, and breathes very slowly. Sometimes it snores! It can wake up quickly if there is danger, such as a flood.

During winter, the bear does not sleep all the time. It may wake up on milder days, and wander about in search of a drink and a snack — and go to the toilet. Then it settles down to snooze again.

Bears rarely share

Bear facts

Bear facts
- The sloth bear lives in India and nearby regions.
- It stays mainly in forests and avoids open places.
- It is quite small compared to other bears, and measures 1.6 metres in length.

Bears nearly always live alone, apart from a mother with her cubs. Sometimes **SLOTH BEARS** gather to share a big feast, such as juicy termites in their mound, or sweet, sticky honey in a wild bees' nest. After the meal, they wander off on their own again.

The sloth bear has long, shaggy fur. There is a white patch on the chest, often shaped like a Y or U.

The sloth bear is quite small, but its claws are very long – each one is probably as large as your whole finger. The front claws are longer than the back ones.

Long claws are excellent for digging up ants, termites and grubs, but not so good for climbing. Sloth bears usually run from enemies rather than climb a tree.

This bear's lips are strong, and it sucks up ants or termites one by one. The sucking is so noisy, it can be heard from 100 metres away!

Hang on, junior!

The baby sloth bear rides 'bear-back' on its mother. She has a special patch of fur there, so the cub can hang on more easily.

Sloth bears are named because they move slowly – just like real sloths. But if they are in danger, they may strike out with their long, sharp claws.

Rare bear

Bear facts

- Giant pandas live in small areas of southwest China.
- Their bamboo forest homes are high in the hills.
- An adult giant panda measures 1.8 metres in length and weighs 100 kilograms.

The **GIANT PANDA** is an extremely rare animal. There are only about 1000 left living in the wild, all in China. This bear is famous for eating just one food – bamboo, a type of fast-growing, woody grass. But sometimes the panda snacks on different foods.

A panda may raid a bird's nest for eggs, or catch a lizard or mouse, or even eat the meat from a dead animal such as a forest pig. But most of its food, 99 meals out of 100, is bamboo.

Bears rarely make noises. Pandas can groan like a whale, bark like a dog and bleat like a sheep! This happens when they try to avoid each other, or when a male and female get together to mate.

People once thought giant pandas were related to raccoons. Scientists now know that they are members of the bear family. These endangered creatures need our help to survive.

Six fingers?

The panda seems to have six fingers. But the extra one is really part of its wrist. It helps it to hold food.

Biggest bears

Bear facts
- Kodiak bears weigh most in autumn, as they feed on plentiful fruits, berries and fish.
- They can sprint at over 30 kilometres an hour – that is faster than most humans!

The brown bears called **KODIAK BEARS** are the biggest land hunters. They can weigh almost one tonne! They live on Kodiak Island, off the south coast of Alaska, in the far northwest of North America. Most of Kodiak Island is a nature reserve where bears and other creatures live and feed in peace.

Tall and small
A Kodiak bear may stand almost twice as high as a person – and weigh ten times as much.

A bear has small front teeth called incisors for nibbling and nipping, and long canine teeth for stabbing and tearing. Its back teeth, or molars, are wide, for chewing.

Bears such as the Kodiak roam a regular area called their home range. They leave smelly droppings and urine, and scratch marks on trees, to tell other bears of their presence.

If two bears meet, they usually ignore each other and go their separate ways. Unless it is the breeding season!

Some bears like ice

Bear facts

- A male polar bear is about 3 metres long and weighs half a tonne.
- As in most bears, the female is smaller, about two-thirds of the male's size.
- Polar bears live all around the Arctic.

The **POLAR BEAR** is one of the biggest bears — almost equally as massive as the brown bear. It is also the fiercest, because it does much more hunting than the other types of bear, and eats far fewer fruits, berries or plants.

The polar bear is at home in the water, as well as on land. It paddles fast with its massive front paws and can swim for many hours.

Polar bears eat many animals, especially seals, small whales, seabirds and their eggs, caribou (reindeer) and even rats!

The baby polar bear is born in midwinter, in a den dug in the snow. It stays there with its mother for three months.

White fur helps to camouflage the polar bear, so it blends in with the ice and snow of its Arctic home. Its thick fur and a layer of fat under its skin keep the bear very warm.

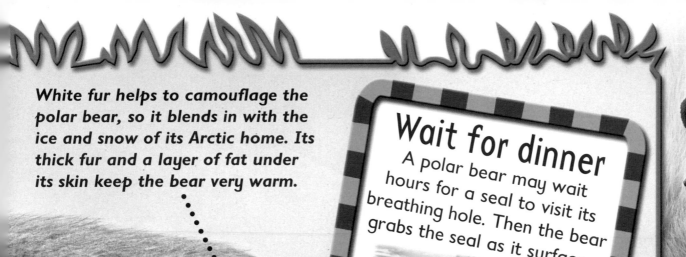

Wait for dinner

A polar bear may wait hours for a seal to visit its breathing hole. Then the bear grabs the seal as it surfaces.

At first, the cub feeds on its mother's milk. From the age of five months it shares its mother's food. Then it begins to hunt for its own meals. By the age of two and a half years, the young bear has left its mother to live alone.

The polar bear cub learns to swim with its mother. Male bears never take part in caring for their cubs. In fact males sometimes try to kill them!

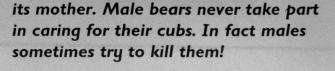

Killers kill!

All whales and dolphins feed on other animals. The **KILLER WHALE** hunts big prey such as seals, albatrosses, and fish as large as you. But sometimes the killer whale makes do with a small fish as a snack.

Dolphin facts

• Killer 'whales' are really the largest members of the dolphin group.

• A big male is about 10 metres long and weighs 10 tonnes.

• Killer whales roam all seas, although they rarely visit the warmest tropics.

• Killer whales are also called orcas.

Wave of death

Some killer whales ride the surf onto the beach, grab a seal and wriggle back into the sea to eat it.

Killer whales 'talk' in clicks and squeaks as they circle their prey.

Killer whales live in groups called pods. The older females are in charge. Their offspring (young) may stay together for 10 to 20 years.

The tall fin on the back is called the dorsal fin. It helps the killer whale to swim straight, without tilting over.

The killer has about 50 teeth, each one almost as big as your hand. They are suited for grabbing and tearing, not chewing.

These massive mammals can swim along at 50 kilometres an hour.

Dolphins like to play

Dolphins often leap from the water and fall back with a splash and crash – because they want to! They seem to play and have fun. But their play could be partly serious. Perhaps these **BOTTLENOSE DOLPHINS** want to attract a partner for breeding. Or they make noise to gather fish into a small area – for dinner!

Dolphin facts

• The bottlenose dolphin grows to about 4 metres long.

• It lives in warmer oceans worldwide.

• It sometimes gathers in huge schools (groups) of over 500.

The dolphin's snout, or beak, is shaped like a round, hard bottle. In its mouth are 100 small, sharp teeth, ready to snap up a meal.

A dolphin's smooth, slippery skin slides through the water at super speed. The bottlenose dolphin races along at 50 kilometres an hour – far faster than a person can run.

Click-click

Dolphins click and squeak, and can hear these sounds bounce back off fish. This is how they find dinner in muddy water or at night.

Bottlenose dolphins can leap more than 6 metres out of the water. But they need a good 'run-up'. They dive down deep, then swim upwards fast, bursting from the surface in a fountain of spray.

The dolphin waves its tail flukes (fins) up and down with great power, to get up to top speed.

Biggest hunter ever!

Whale facts

- Sperm whales live in all oceans, even cold polar waters.
- The bull (male) grows to about 20 metres long and 50 tonnes in weight.
- The cow (female) is about 15 metres long and half as heavy.

Great meat-eating dinosaurs like *Tyrannosaurus* were huge, but the **SPERM WHALE** is ten times bigger – the largest hunter that has ever lived. It is also one of the deepest divers in the whale group, heading down over 3000 metres into the cold, black ocean depths.

This huge whale has a huge appetite. It hunts big fish, octopus and even the dreaded giant squid.

Sperm whales can hold their breath for more than one hour, as they dive down and down. They use clicks of sound, which they hear bouncing back off nearby objects, to find their prey in the darkness.

The sperm whale's back fin is just a small hump, with even smaller humps behind.

Small giants!

There are three kinds of sperm whale. The pygmy one is medium-sized. The dwarf sperm whale is 'tiny' yet still twice as big as a person!

There are about 50 cone-shaped teeth in the very narrow lower jaw – but no teeth at all in the upper jaw.

Some dolphins can hardly see

Dolphin facts

- The susu grows to more than 2.5 metres in length.
- It weighs up to 90 kilograms.
- Female susus are slightly larger than males.
- Another local name for this dolphin is the bhulan.

There are about 38 kinds of dolphins. But only five types live all their lives in fresh water, in rivers and lakes. The **SUSU**, also known as the Ganges River dolphin, is from the Indian region. It is very shy and extremely endangered.

Like all whales and dolphins, the susu's flippers are paddle-shaped for swimming and steering.

The susu comes up for air often, every minute or two.

Whales and dolphins swim by arching the body to swish the tail flukes up and down (fish have upright tail fins and bend their bodies from side to side).

Safe or not?
Most sharks have triangular fins, while most dolphins have swept-back ones.

The susu has tiny, deep-set eyes. These can only pick out blurs of light and darkness. The dolphin finds its way mainly by sound clicks.

Susus have more than 120 small, sharp teeth. They work like spikes to grab fish, shellfish, worms and crabs near the riverbed and in the mud.

Whales hate beaches

Dolphin facts

• Pilot whales live in all oceans except for the far north and south.

• Males are up to 7 metres long and 2 tonnes in weight.

• Females are smaller, but live longer – up to 60 years.

PILOT WHALES, like most whales and dolphins, usually stay away from the shore. But sometimes they follow prey into the shallows. Then they are in danger of being stranded – stuck on the beach, where they would soon die.

Pilot 'whales' are really large dolphins. They are also called 'blackfish'.

The forehead is very rounded, or bulbous, giving the nickname 'melon-head'.

Stick to mother

A baby whale or dolphin is called a calf. It feeds on its mother's milk and stays near her all the time. A new baby pilot whale is 1.6 metres long.

Pilot whales usually hunt in deep water, diving down 500 metres or more. They hold their breath for over 15 minutes as they chase squid, octopus and fish.

Pilot whales live in groups called schools, which can number over 100. Sometimes they swim with other dolphins, or perhaps with small whales such as minkes.

Each pilot whale in the group makes its own special clicks and whistles, which the others recognize.

If one pilot whale is ill or injured, the others gather round. They try to protect and look after it.

Whales wail!

Whale facts

- The humpback is one of the bigger whales, about 15 metres long and weighing up to 40 tonnes.
- It lives in all the world's oceans.
- Humpbacks migrate to colder waters in summer, and back to warmer regions for winter.

All whales and dolphins make clicks, squeaks, squeals, moans, wails and other sounds. These travel fast and far through the water. The male **HUMPBACK WHALE** is one of the champion singers. He is probably trying to attract a female with his loud, long 'love-song'.

Humpbacks have lots of lumps and bumps on their heads. Hard-shelled sea creatures called barnacles also live there.

As the humpback sings, he arches his body so that his head and tail droop downwards. He does not swim, but hangs in mid-water.

The song lasts for 40 minutes or more. Then the humpback sings it all again – and again, for up to 20 hours!

Each male has his own song. It carries huge distances through the ocean – 100 kilometres or more. Also, he changes it slightly from one year to the next.

The humpback's flippers are massive, up to 5 metres long, with lumps along the front edge.

Mouthful of sea

The humpback gulps a vast mouthful of water and squeezes it out again, trapping small animals inside for its food.

Porpoises blow bubbles

Porpoise facts

Porpoise facts
- There are six kinds of porpoises around the world.
- The harbour porpoise is about 1.7 metres long and 65 kilograms in weight.

The **HARBOUR PORPOISE** is a close cousin of whales and dolphins. Like them, and us, it is a mammal. This means it has warm blood and it breathes air. But its nose is not at the front of the face — it's on the top of the head! This breathing opening is called a blowhole.

All porpoises, whales and dolphins hold their breath under the water, although a few bubbles of air may escape from the blowhole.

As its name suggests, the harbour porpoise sometimes comes into ports and harbours, especially at night. It noses about among the rubbish on the seabed, for bits of old fish and other scraps that people throw away.

The harbour porpoise usually hunts alone in shallow waters near the shore. It feasts mainly on fish and shellfish.

180

Lots of teeth

Dolphins and porpoises have many small, sharp teeth for spiking slippery fish and stabbing squirming squid.

When these animals return to the surface, they blow out the stale air, making a spray that looks like a fountain!

Baby whales are big

Whale facts

- A full-grown gray whale is 15 metres long and 35 tonnes in weight.
- Gray whales live along the coasts of the North Pacific Ocean.

Just like other mammals, whale and dolphin mothers give birth to babies and feed them on milk. The newborn **GRAY WHALE** is one of the world's biggest babies — 5 metres long and weighing half a tonne!

The mother whale's teats are on her rear underside, towards her tail. She lies on her side so her baby can breathe easily while it is feeding.

The mother gray whale is pregnant (when her baby is growing inside her womb) for 13 months.

The baby whale sometimes partly lies on its mother, for a rest or a piggy-back ride. The mother helps it to reach the surface regularly, for breaths of fresh air.

Pesky pests

A whale is like a moving rock, where barnacles, limpets and other creatures attach themselves and grow.

The young whale, or calf, depends on its mother for milk and protection for 9 months. Then it is old enough to fend for itself.

Whales may fight

Whale facts
- Narwhals live in the far north, among the icebergs of the Arctic Ocean.
- A narwhal is about 4.5 metres long and weighs 1.5 tonnes.

In some types of whales, the males fight each other at breeding time. Male **NARWHALS** show off their long tusks, waving them in the air at each other, and even using them like swords in a fencing fight.

The male which wins the contest is most likely to mate with a female and become a father. However he does not take any care of the baby. Only female whales and dolphins care for their young.

The narwhal's tusk is not used for eating. These whales feed by powerfully sucking in small animals, with their bendy lips and tongue.

Whitest whale

The narwhal's close cousin in far-north waters is the beluga. It is all-white, and is also the noisiest whale — and it can make faces!

The narwhal's corkscrew-like tusk is a very long, sharp tooth called an incisor. It grows from the upper jaw, out through the skin, and up to 3 metres long. Usually only the male has the tusk.

Narwhals eat many kinds of fish and shellfish, especially from the seabed. They also make a wide range of loud noises which can even be heard above the surface.

Blues are biggest!

Whale facts

- The blue whale is a true giant, almost 30 metres long and 150 tonnes in weight.
- It lives in all the world's oceans.
- Blues swim to the far north or south for summer, and back to the tropics for winter.

The **BLUE WHALE** is the largest creature in the world. Yet its main food, the shrimplike shellfish called krill, are each smaller than your finger. Luckily the blue whale eats more than one million of them every day.

Great whales such as the blue whale have no teeth. Their mouths contain long strips of a tough, springy substance called baleen or 'whalebone'.

When people hunted blue whales, they became very rare. Now these great whales are protected by laws. They are slowly increasing their numbers again.

But many small whales, dolphins and porpoises are still hunted. Others are trapped in fishing nets and drown, or they are poisoned by pollution. All of these amazing sea mammals need our care and protection.

Whale out of water

It is hard to imagine how big a blue whale is, unless you lift it out of the water and take it home – which would be quite difficult!

The blue whale opens its mouth wide, takes a gulp of water and krill, then closes its mouth to squeeze out the water through its baleen. The brush-edged strips work like a massive comb, to filter the water and trap the krill inside. The whale then licks off the krill and swallows them.

Index

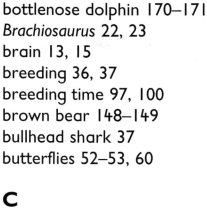

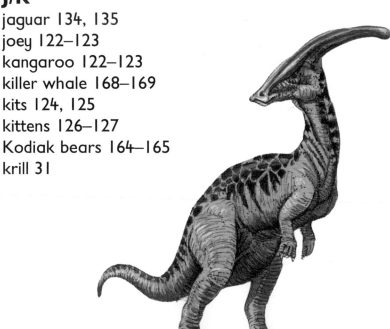

The publishers would like to thank the following artists
for contributing to this book:

Baby Animals: Ian Jackson
Bears: Andrea Morandi
Big Cats: Ian Jackson
Bugs: Richard Draper
Crocodiles: Steve Roberts
Dinosaurs: Chris Buzer
Owls: Andrea Morandi
Sharks: John Butler
Whales & Dolphins: Syd Brak